JAPANESE MYTHOLOGY

A fascinating introduction to Japanese mythology, myths, legends and deities

By

IACOBELLIS EDIZIONI

IACOBELLIS EDIZIONI

Table of Contents

Introduction

The link between myth and life is complicated for many modern Japanese. Myth is made up of stories about both hazy and tangible beings and objects. It also includes accepted, often indisputable ideas regarding the Japanese people's origins, habits, and culture. Few Japanese people will acknowledge "believing" in such legends. They simply present themselves as if they do. To make matters even more complicated, religion and ritual, as well as household and national rituals, intertwine in subtle and unanticipated ways.

Myths, as defined in this book, are at the crossroads of various narrative styles. On the one hand, there is the folktale category, which includes oral stories that are told traditionally. They are frequently legendary (discussing deities, causes for events, and morals) and occasionally just for fun. Many of these folktales were gathered by Japanese folklorists, especially in the early half of the twentieth century, when oral traditions began to fade as radio, television, and other forms of entertainment became more prevalent. The ghost story is another popular narrative style in Japan. Ghost stories were typically derived from a Buddhist tradition concerned with the afterlife and the consequences of one's actions during one's lifetime. They were traditionally recounted in the middle of the heat to send a shiver down the listener's back (a simple type of air conditioning!). A third prominent tale form is "official" myths, which are frequently documented by or at the request of those in positions of authority to create charters for political and social situations. All of these elements contribute to the mythology of a society.

This book's mythology acknowledges various sources, both oral and written, folk and elite. Many "alternative" versions have been omitted or only briefly discussed in order to provide a coherent image for a non-specialized audience.

This book provides the readers with the basic inaugurating knowledge about Japanese Mythology. It contains an informative and interesting set of details regarding myths in Japan.

This book is meant for beginners to let them get a grip on the basics of Japanese Mythology so that they may lead their way to understanding Japanese culture.

Chapter 1-Japan and Myths: Overview

Gods are said to be born from the eyes or nostrils of other gods in Japanese mythology. They tie the knot with their brothers or sisters. Their rectums are used to make food. They become enraged and begin chopping each other up.

One deity rips off her clothes and dances in front of the other gods, who all burst out laughing.

However, none of this is exactly what the Japanese people demand from themselves. In reality, Japanese people are known for their conservatism and reverence for civility, moderation, and cleanliness. However, in Japanese mythology, outrageous behavior is rather common. At best, the gods' behavior is weird, and at worst, it's repulsive. It generally does not set a direct example of how to behave for humans. The message sometimes appears to be that the gods lack human characteristics. They are not human, despite the fact that they are described as such.

In many creation stories, gods, for example, live in a realm distinct from the one in which people live. Gods live in these myths in a world that existed before existence, before the sun and moon, and before land and water. It portrays a time before natural laws and human rules and conventions existed.

Japan's name, Nihon or Nippon, is derived from Chinese characters that indicate "sun's origin." The sun comes up from the east; hence Japan is to the east of China. According to Japanese mythology, the Japanese people are the offspring of Amaterasu, the sun goddess.

Japan's flag is white, with a solid red circle in the center. The red circle represents the sun.

Shinto, Japan's national religion, is centered on the worship of various gods and spirits; Shinto literally means "way of the kami." Gods are known as kami in Japanese, and they are said to inhabit all living things, including humans, as well as nonliving objects such as rocks, waterfalls, trees, and buildings. Many of Japan's mythological myths focus on Amaterasu, the sun goddess.

1.1 Japan

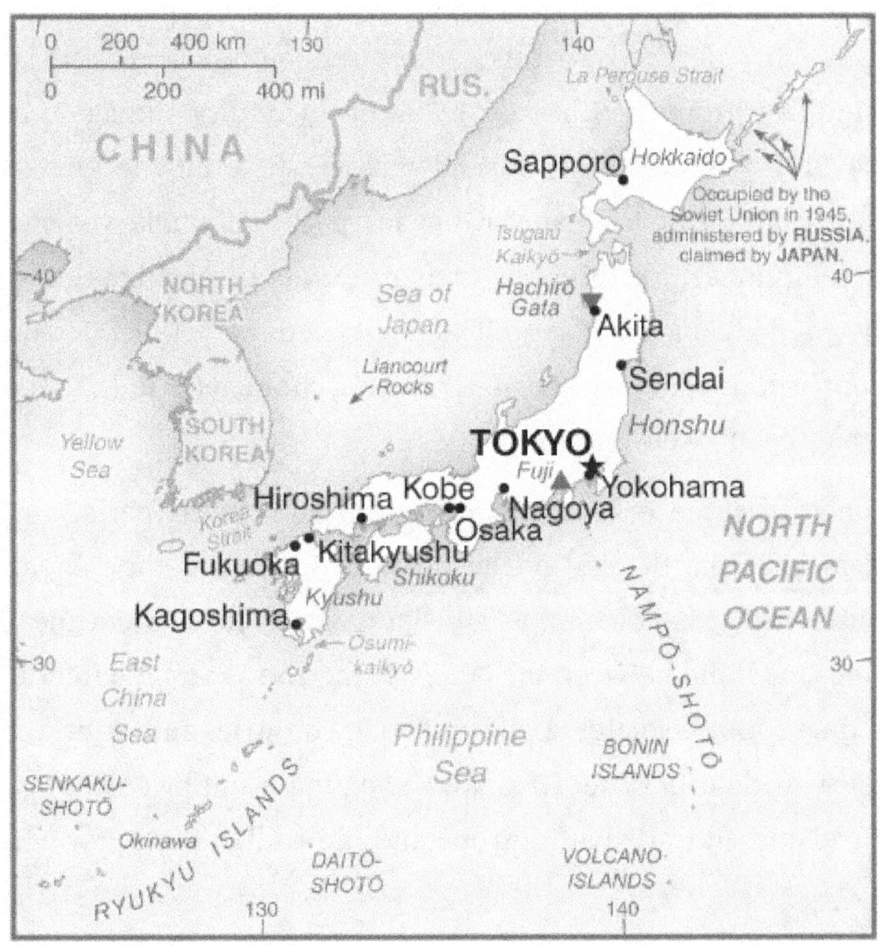

The most important thing to know about Japan is that it is an island nation with few natural resources: an archipelago of small, mountainous islands. Unlike many modern countries, Japan is racially homogeneous, with practically everyone sharing the same ancestry and customs.

Throughout history, the Japanese have taken elements from other cultures and adapted them to their own culture. In the 500s, they learned writing, structured administration, and Buddhism from the Chinese. In the 19th century and again in the 20th century, they learned techniques from the United States and Europe. Whatever they learn—how to make vehicles or cell phones, for example, or figure skate or play baseball—they quickly master it as well as, if not better than, the person from whom they learned it. This is a characteristic that the Japanese are well-known for.

Times of intense learning have alternated with periods of seclusion from the rest of the world in Japan's history. Japan makes use of its location as an island nation throughout these times. As it did between the outset of the 1600s and the middle of the 1800s, it isolates itself from other countries and embraces its own identity. The Tokugawa shogunate outlawed foreign travel and all trade with Europe and the United States for 250 years.

Japan attempted to reject Buddhism and reinstate Shinto in the nineteenth century after adopting Buddhism as a religion and combining it with Shinto, the native Japanese faith. This was partly in response to Japan's national doors being pried open by the West: Commodore Matthew Perry landed with a fleet of ships in 1853 and compelled Japan to open economic links with the U.S. and eventually Europe. After being reinstated to power after years of military dictatorships, Emperor Meiji thought it was time to modernize. He intended Japan to thrive economically in a more industrialized world, but he didn't want the Japanese to lose their cultural identity. As a result, there was a period of intense nationalism and the government's adoption of traditional Japanese mythology. One of these legends claimed that the emperor was a divinity and a direct descendant of the goddess of the sun. This myth reinforced the idea that Japan was a superior nation due to its ancestors. This tale was once interpreted to suggest that the emperor had the authority to dominate the entire universe.

1.2 Industrialized Japan

Japanese firms thrived, as did the country's economy. Japan's industrialization was quick. It effectively transitioned from an agrarian nation to one with the world's largest gross national product (GNP) in just a few years. Then, during World War II, Japan fought alongside Germany against the U.S. and Russia on the side of the Axis powers. On December 7, 1941, Japan made a dramatic entry into the war by bombing the U.S. naval facility at Pearl Harbor. The bombing killed over 2,000 American sailors and drew the United States into the conflict. Only until the United States retaliated by dropping atomic bombs on the Japanese cities of Hiroshima and Nagasaki did Japan surrender. Shinto was abolished as the official national religion after Emperor Hirohito relinquished his claim to be a god.

Many people are still writing books to figure out how the Japanese were able to industrialize with such speed and efficiency. Despite this, the Japanese continued to relate their myths to successive generations and to visit Shinto shrines and Buddhist temples throughout all eras when the state declared a religion.

1.3 The Japanese Myth

The myth of Japan is one of the most common beliefs held by the Japanese. In this view, Japan is an island nation, distinct in terms of culture and geography, mysterious and homogeneous.

Of course, this is part of the Great Tradition, and it is what has been passed down to us in the form of written materials, such as the Kojiki and Nihonshoki writings. In modern Japan, the Great Tradition of Japanese legend is very much alive. The majority of Japanese people still believe in one or more of the following:

- The Japanese language is distinctive, with just a few traces of other languages;

- Japanese culture, especially the Japanese style of thinking, is unfathomable to non-native speakers. This is especially true in Japanese communication, which is heavily reliant on unspoken, felt emotions transferred between those who share them: the Japanese people.

- The Japanese people have a unique origin.

- Japan's cultural evolution has been essentially unrelated to global changes.

And many will agree that the Japanese people's set of physical characteristics is homogeneous and unique. As a result, during the last five decades, publications have been published in Japanese, claiming that the Japanese are unique because of their intestine length, hair color, blood type, or physical brain anatomy.

It just so happens that none of these points of view are correct. These myths persist, however, because the elite—the bureaucrats, academia, religious officials, even showbiz celebrities and foreign journalists—repeat these fictional facts as if they were factual. To some extent, they are, but only when numerous criteria are added. They are mythical realities that derive from and sustain the existence of many of the specific "narrative" myths we will analyze here for our purposes in analyzing Japanese mythology. To do so, we'll look at some of the characteristics of Japanese society that give rise to Japanese mythology.

1.4 Language and Writing

The Japanese language is an important part of Japanese culture that is crucial to myths. Japanese is a member of the Ural-Altaic language family, which also includes Korean and Manchu. These languages are agglutinative, which means that words are modified by meaningless particles to signify things like verbs, politeness levels, tense, and so on. Japanese, on the other hand, is written in ideographic kanji (Chinese characters). Because the Chinese do not have agglutinations, the Japanese developed two sets of syllabaries (characters indicating a consonant and a vowel) to write these agglutinations (one of these, katakana, was invented to make reading Buddhist scriptures easier for women who were thought to be too weak-minded to read proper Chinese characters). As a result, many Japanese concepts are stated using only two words: one of Japanese origin and the other of Chinese origin. Furthermore, while each Chinese character has a distinct meaning, its "reading"—the sound it denotes—can have a variety of interpretations in Japanese.

All of this has ramifications in Japanese mythology. The names of mythological beings and things, as well as their qualities, can be generated from different readings/interpretations of their names, locations, or deeds. A name that had one meaning in the on Yomi (Chinese reading) of a word may be read as if it were Kun Yomi (Japanese reading), and the meaning is put into the sound. Here's an illustration: The three monkeys, Hear No Evil, See No Evil, and Speak No Evil, are well-known. They are linked to the road kami, Sarutahiko-no-kami, in Japanese mythology. Saru means monkey in Japanese, while ta indicates rice paddy. The kami's name is written in Chinese characters using the characters for monkey and field, which sound similar to the kami's name. This links the deity to monkeys, despite the fact that there is no such link in the Kojiki or the Nihonshoki, where Sarutahiko is referenced. The verb suffix -Saru or -zaru is the negative imperative suffix of a verb in old Japanese ("do not..."). Thus, the exhortation to hear no evil, see no evil and speak no evil, which is likely from a Buddhist source, can be visualized as three monkeys, thus linking these three monkeys with Sarutahiko.

Chapter 2-Japanese Traditions and Mythology

In at least two instances, the term "Japanese mythology" is misleading. To begin with, rather than having single cohesive mythology, the Japanese people have a plethora of them. There are a variety of mythical traditions, some of which have been written down (and are useful to policymakers and ideologues), and others that are spoken among friends and dismissed by specialists as "folk traditions" rather than "real" mythology. Small village mythologies and the myths of the Japanese island's minority peoples—the Ainu and Ryukyuans—are not often considered "truly" Japanese or "properly" mythical. Second, even "true" Japanese mythology—whatever that means—is a collection of indigenous mythologies as well as mythologies from other cultures, mostly India and China, but also the West.

To make matters worse, the phrase myth can be perplexing in and of itself. Myths are made up of two components for our needs. The section about telling stories is one of the elements.

Myths nearly invariably include supernatural elements (i.e., the intervention of powerful, independent beings). These tales can range in length from epics to short anecdotes. It's tough to tell the difference between myths, folklore, ghost stories, and fairy tales in this context.

Myths, on the other hand, have a second component: They usually have an intellectual component that gives people's lives structure. Individuals or an entire civilization could be involved. Myths are stories that people tell themselves to explain who they are, what they're doing, and why they're doing it. Though no single myth can achieve everything, the corpus of myth, however conflicting and fractured, provides people with a list of explanations for how things happen and why and how they came to be as the result of a long (and thus respectable, worth sticking to and defending) process. Many of the myths discussed in this book follow a typical narrative pattern: Somebody did something in the foggy past under certain circumstances that have social, physical, material, and/or ideological effects that we can see now. Other myths, on the other hand, lack a narrative. They are descriptions of features of the universe, civilization, and history in verse, sculpture, art, or architecture. To give an example, one of the most important Buddhist figures, Kannon, has no "stories" in the traditional sense. There are, however, extensive descriptions of her characteristics and personality. Kannon also appears as a savior and supporter in a variety of myth stories concerning various people.

In more practical aspects, Japanese myth has played a crucial role, particularly as a social and political charter. The Takahashi and the Imbe families competed for the job of imperial family chef in the early ninth century. Each used their clan myths as evidence to support their assertions. In the 1980s, a Japanese government minister used the myth of Japanese uniqueness as a reason for restricting meat imports. Although none of these parties were "believed" by their listeners, the myths stated were regarded as powerful and persuasive arguments.

2.1 Great Traditions and Little Traditions

Yanagita Kunio, and subsequently Origuchi Shinobu, began collecting peasant and common folklore in the early twentieth century, which Yanagita feared was swiftly vanishing. Yanagita, in particular, believed that this folklore was the "original" and "true" folklore of the Japanese people and hence the core of the conventional and genuine Japaneseness that gave birth to the Japanese country. Many of the tales collected by Yanagita and Origuchi were localized to certain places, stories that did not always mirror what was being taught and retold in schools as becoming Japanese traditions, at least as per the government. Surprisingly, several of these tales contradicted existing beliefs recorded in massive Japanese tradition collections such as the Kojiki and the Nihonshoki. In the eighteenth century, these were reissued and republicized as a component of an ideological drive to "renovate" Japanese society. It's helpful to look to a set of terminology attributed to American anthropologist Robert Redfield to clarify these inconsistencies. Redfield, who worked in Mexico and was a contemporary of Yanagita, invented the terms "Little Traditions" and "Great Tradition," which will be useful here.

"Little Traditions" are collections of local beliefs and behaviors found in all human groups but are especially common in societies that are largely self-contained, if not secluded. Little Traditions differ from one community to the next, are very adaptable and dynamic, and are rarely documented since individuals who repeat them are frequently illiterate. They concentrate on these communities' immediate concerns: family, social duties, agriculture, and healthcare. The mythology of ordinary people is embodied in the Little Traditions.

In contrast, a nation's or culture's "Great Tradition" is more likely to be written down, printed in books, legislated, and almost preserved. It is dominated by the elite (who are generally well-educated and always strong) and serves their interests: glorifying the nation, religion, and culture in terms that they, the elite, define for their own ends.

Little and Great Traditions have a dynamic interaction. The Great Tradition aims to rally individuals for the purposes of the entire civilization that they lead through its major supporters, the literate elites. Local legends and myths are incorporated into the Great Tradition to the extent that they can be used to buttress the elite and national mythologies. Little Traditions feed into the Great Tradition, but they frequently deal with topics that aren't important to it—hunger, local nationalism, producers' and farmers' concerns—or are even antagonistic to it, such as ideas of revolt. Little Traditions, on the other hand, may appropriate and alter myths from the Great Tradition for their own goals.

2.2 Little and Great Traditions in the Japanese Context

Localism has always lived in harmony uncomfortably with "Japanism" in the Japanese setting. That is to say, most personal concern was concentrated on, and the greatest emotional commitment was provided to the local community—the buraku (hamlet) and the i.e. (household). Except for those in power, the greater community—the nation or the han (feudal domain)—was of little importance to most people. As a result of this duality, the central government (when it was dominant and able to do so) went to great lengths to "nationalize" local myths in order to foster and develop a nation rather than a collection of disparate communities. It's not strange, then, that the identical deity may perform multiple functions and have multiple identities and titles or that diverse deity will be merged into one, and separate mythologies will be "amalgamated" into one narrative that suits the purposes of those in power.

2.3 Japanese Traditions from Outside Sources

A variety of external sources affected Japanese traditions, including mythological ones. Two of these are widely recorded and relatively straightforward to track because they are literate cultural practices. Both India and China made significant contributions to Japanese mythology, mostly through the medium of Buddhism. There is also evidence of two more traditions, both of which are less well recorded and significantly more diffuse: Ainu mythology is the crystallization and manifestation of traditions present in several surrounding cultures to the north and northwest of Japan, such as the Okhotskian and Tungus,,, cultures. It's also possible to see parallels between Japanese myths—for instance, the legend of the land's creators, the brother-sister merging of Izanagi and Izanami—and myths from the proto-Polynesian civilizations of the island chains that stretch southward from Japan, through the Taiwan, Ryukyus, and the Philippines, where this myth (among others) is retold in many variations.

2.3.1 Chinese Sources

The mythology of adjacent China has had a massive impact on Japanese mythology. Chinese mythology was made up of a fusion of two different cultures. One was the indigenous belief in gods (shin), who were grouped in vast assemblages of heavenly bureaucrats, princes, and generals, commanded by a supreme Jade Emperor, or Celestial Emperor, who controlled the skies with righteousness and compassion, as the earthly Chinese emperor was intended to do on earth. A vast number of local deities and saints were absorbed into this cosmos in the shape of heavenly officials, some of whom were historical figures with verifiable existence whose virtues pleased their contemporaries.

The other tradition was Buddhism, which was itself a synthesis of earlier Hindu traditions as well as various Central Asian and even Persian mythologies. Buddhism brought new deities and conceptions, as well as new sages and saints, to China, and they, too, took on the shape of a celestial bureaucracy, coexisting with or identifying with the native one.

Chinese ideas of the mythological realm, like all mythology, were based on people's perceptions and understandings of the social reality around them. The imperial governance system was a fundamental social characteristic of the old Chinese world. Although the emperor was sovereign, he was supposed to lead by virtue, and he was, in theory, the head of a bureaucracy whose members were appointed on merit. In formal terms, all males were given the opportunity to become officials through a system of severe (and difficult!) assessments. In theory, even the poorest farmer's son could become the kingdom's chief minister. As a result, official jobs within the celestial government's bureaucracy are represented in Chinese mythology. This bureaucracy was organized into divisions and bureaus, just like the imperial government of the material world.

Japan never developed a merit-based examination system, despite adhering to portions of the Confucian ethic. Clan and family affiliation, as well as the ruler's relationship, were significantly more essential. Furthermore, outlying areas of the Japanese polity owed a true duty to their respective clans and later feudal lords, despite always expressing strong loyalty to the emperor.

This is reflected in the mythological distinctions between the two social systems. Because Japan lacked a comparable governmental system, much of the justification for a person's deification went when the Japanese acquired mythological characters from China (for example, the translation of Ch'ung-Chuan into Shoki Demon-queller). As a result, mythological characters in Japan have distinct levels of significance and even different responsibilities than their Chinese counterparts.

2.3.2 Buddhism and Indian sources

Long before Japan emerged as a nation, India had a flourishing literate culture. The previous legendary heritage of Hinduism was absorbed and developed by Indian Buddhism. The pantheon of mighty, well-defined gods was mentioned in Indian mythology. Numerous of Hinduism's most important deities—Brahma the Creator, Vishnu the Sustainer, Indra the Fort-

Breaker, and even many demons—were recast as Buddhist figures, lesser than the Buddhas but nevertheless powerful and deserving of respect. These figures and deities were conveyed to Japan via China and became protagonists in Japanese mythology as well, with Japanese names and traits but clearly derived from a rich Hindu and Indian history. Similarly, sociological variations between India and Japan—for example, the lack of a caste system—meant that imported deities were located in different contexts than in their native place, with matching differences in the mythology related to them.

Chapter 3-Outlying Myth Complexes

The idea of a politically and culturally homogenous Japan was promoted by Japanese national and imperial mythology. This represented the central elite's goals and interests while ignoring or blurring the concerns of local communities and the Little Traditions. However, the Japanese people are not as identical as the authorities claimed. Two other separate cultures—possibly the only two surviving remains of a richer and more diverse cultural fabric that existed in the Japanese islands prior to Yamato's rise to power—retain certain aspects of their cultural past, including mythology. These two cultures—the Ainu of the north and the Ryukyuans of the south—are noteworthy not only for their own sakes but also for the relative light they reflect on Japanese (here understood to imply Yamato tradition) mythology.

3.1 Okinawa and the Ryukyu Islands

The Ryukyu island chain, of which Okinawa is the largest island, is found in Okinawa Prefecture, which is situated in the southern region of Japan. The Yamato tongue and culture are distinct from those of the native peoples and should not be confused with them (that is, standard Japanese). Prior to its conquest by the Japanese Satsuma clan in the 16th and 17th centuries, Okinawa functioned as a sovereign kingdom in its own right. It was a cultural bridge between China and Japan, as well as a cultural melting pot due to the fact that it was affected by both China and Japan. Up until this century, many aspects of Okinawan culture and religion had been kept apart from one another. The Ryukyu Islands span a distance of approximately 400 kilometers, stretching from the most southern point of

Kyushu to the northernmost shore of Taiwan. The island of Okinawa is located in the middle of the Japanese archipelago and stretches for a total of seventy miles.

In many instances, what has been claimed to as a Ryukyuan myth was actually a rewriting done by a scholar from mainland Japan looking for some kind of Okinawan-Japanese connection, typically to prove Japan's superiority.

Origin stories are the most common type of tale that is told again and again, despite the fact that even these myths are frequently simplified and localized. The majority of Ryukyuans have a religious upbringing, and as a result, they recognize the importance of taking part in rituals and performing the responsibilities associated with them. On the other hand, the unequivocal enunciation of the gods that they worship is neither the focal point of their religion nor an essential component of its practice. The importance of proper ceremonial behavior, which is deeply embedded in everyday life and interpersonal interactions in Ryukyuan society, cannot be overstated.

Agriculture for subsistence and fishing were the two primary industries that supported the Ryukyuan economy. Sho Hashi, in the year 1429, created a unified kingdom out of the formerly independent petty polities that existed on the islands. This may have been done under the influence of Chinese envoys. One of his successors, Sho Shin, reinforced these conquests and built a Confucian-based government. This government forbade the carrying of guns and institutionalized the divide between nobles and commoners.

Sho Shin ruled from 1477 until his death in 1526. Late in the sixteenth century, the growing power of the Satsuma domain in southern Japan brought the Okinawan kingdom closer to Japan than to China's orbit. The following century saw the Okinawan kingdom become an integral part of the Satsuma domain.

In contrast to the Japanese populace found on the major islands, virtually all academics agree that Ryukyuans do not have the slightest interest in mythology. Discussions of folklore and mythology appear to excite the interest of the average Okinawan because mythological figures tend to be vague and ill-defined and because these topics are often discussed.

In addition to this, the Ryukyuan religion is one of the few religions in the world that is focused primarily on women: All of the senior ritual experts, including priests and mediums, are women. Women make up the majority of the ritual specialist community. It is not easy to determine whether this is a holdover from an earlier matriarchal form of religion or simply a peculiar aspect of Ryukyuan culture.

In Okinawan mythology, the Kang is considered to be the most significant figure. It is believed that these are relatively comparable to humans, albeit somewhat more powerful. They are represented as people donning Chinese robes and headgear, which is a costume worn by Okinawa's nobility. They are depicted as Chinese. As long as the rituals are performed as prescribed and people behave "properly" in their dealings with one another and the sacred woods and caves in which the Kang make their homes, the Kang is essentially unconcerned with political matters (or, rather, pass through on their way to the prosaic world). The Kang is a formidable race that possesses abilities that humans do not. In the event that the ceremonies are not carried out, they will become a hindrance to human life.

Despite this, human actions and trickery have the potential to manipulate and even fool them. The mythology that is expressed contains a few different categories that can be broken down further. The superior group is known as the ting-nu-Kang or the heavenly Kang. These, much like the Japanese kami, have an ill-defined sense of their own superiority. Unjang (kang of sea), tiida-kang (solar kang) and miiji-nu-kang (kang of water) are among them. Similar to how there are different types of Kang in the Japanese system, there are multiple types of local Kang, such as paddy Kang, well Kang, and home Kang.

Occupational Kang includes people who work in the fishing industry, such as fishermen, people who make fishing nets, and people who build boats. The fourth group consists of the futuki, sometimes known as ancestors; they have the potential to act as a mediator between living people and the Kang. Few Okinawans are capable of recognizing any of these ideas, and even fewer care to differentiate between them. All of these ideas are vague and unclear. In the view of the Ryukyuans, it is sufficient to act appropriately and to make the Nuru offerings (village priestesses).

Despite the lack of clarity surrounding this period, the beginning of legendary history is considered to be the Age of Heaven.

According to a different telling of the same stories, the two individuals descended to the earth with various types of building materials, including stones, dirt, trees, and plants, with which they contained the waters and erected the islands that make up the archipelago (in the Chuzan Seikan). Without ever having sexual contact with one another, they gave birth to three children: the first ruler (a son), the first priestess, and the first farmer (again, a son).

Amaikyu and Shinerikyu, two Kang siblings, were commanded by the heavenly Kang (or, in other versions, by Nirai Kang, the heavenly creator deity) to establish the land and the people that lived on it during that time period. The ting-nu-Kang is also known as Nirai Kang. They descended from heaven and fashioned the legendary paradise of Kudaka Island out of the sea's crashing waves.

After a number of generations, a human being who was a descendant of these early humans was born. Tenteishi, as he was known, was a man who divided people into four categories: monarchs, aristocratic farmers, high priestesses, and village priestesses.

Among the high priestesses, Tenteishi placed the most importance. Each of his five children assumed responsibility for one of these responsibilities. The population was large at the time, and they traveled across the ocean to establish a settlement at Seefa Utaki, also known as the sacred grove of Seefa, on the southern coast of Okinawa. Seefa Utaki is still considered to be Okinawa's most important pilgrimage site.

In every village or community, there is a specific location known as a take where the local priestess goes to commune with the Kang. Because of the way the cosmos is designed, men in Ryukyuan communities hold temporal authority, while their sisters wield the spiritual power that helps to uphold and sustain the men in their communities. The same can be said for the majority of different families. The female-male system was established with the establishment of the unified Okinawan kingdom in the early fifteenth century (the kingdom also administered, to varying degrees, the neighboring islands), and the central government was responsible for teaching and appointing village Nuru (priestesses).

There are two separate spheres of influence for the Ryukyuans: The majority of people have an interest in learning more about the first that of humans, which is to say, the regular world. On the other hand, the Kang domain is not well defined, it is widely spread, and it is little understood. Kang has the power to manifest in the regular world, despite the fact that their home is in that domain. At least as far as humans are concerned, the gateways between the two realms are the sacred trees (utaki), springs, and caverns that offer access to the other realm. Information about individual and family activities ultimately makes its way to the Kang through the hearth. This is the most important factor.

The expansive creation story that was recorded on Okinawa's main island is reproduced on a number of other Ryukyuan islands, albeit with "local" rather than "national" referents this time around. Ouwehand related a story that was very similar to this one but on the island of Hateruma. In this version, Okinawa was not mentioned. The foundation story of brother-sister founder deities can also be found further north, in the Japanese foundation myth, as well as further south, in Taiwan and the

Philippines. Additionally, this story can be found further south, in Taiwan and the Philippines. Additionally, this story can be found further north, in Japan.

3.2 Ainu

The Ainu culture is the other of Japan's original cultures, which has been almost completely assimilated by Yamato culture. They populated northern Honshu and the island of Hokkaido throughout Japan's early history, speaking a language separate from Japanese. As a result of the Yamato kingdom's expansion before and throughout the Heian period, they (or a nearly related culture known to the Japanese as Emishi) gradually integrated into the broader Japanese population of Honshu. By the Kamakura period, Ainu culture in northern Honshu had all but vanished, leaving only place names and cultural effects that could not be pinpointed. In Hokkaido and the southern Sakhalin islands, Ainu culture thrived as an independent civilization. When Hokkaido was opened to Japanese colonization in the nineteenth century, the Ainu were once again under demographic, cultural, and political pressure from the Japanese. As a unique civilization, they are all but vanished now. Some components of the culture are preserved in remnant communities, particularly for the tourist trade. Around 18,000 people today can trace their ancestors to the Ainu.

The Ainu were part of a much broader circumpolar arctic civilization. Until the Japanese compelled them to renounce traditional habits and become full-time farmers, their economy was based on a combination of gathering and hunting with some subsistence millet farming. Sea-borne trade was an essential part of their political economy, and their big, clinker-built vessels traversed the waterways between the northeast Asian islands and presumably the mainland as well. They were similar to their Asian cultural ancestors in Siberia and Tunguska, as well as the Northwest Coast cultures of North America, in this regard.

The Ainu, a warlike tribe, fought their Sea People neighbors — most likely members of the Okhotskian Culture, who occupied the island chains to the north of Hokkaido — and then the

Japanese, who only defeated them in the eighteenth century. Many Ainu mythology related to battles with the Sea People or the Japanese's betrayal when the Ainu turned to them for valuable items like lacquerware and metalwork.

The Ainu were divided into small bands or villages of roughly a hundred people, each divided into multiple houses in terms of politics. These groups established a kotan, or realm, in which they, and only they, may hunt, fish, and gather. Each kotan was centered on a river valley, with mountains rising between them. According to the evidence in the sagas, raiding and fighting was extremely prevalent. Communities were mainly isolated from one another, yet the requirement to marry outside one's matrilineage resulted in some inter-communal contact and, as a result, cultural uniformity.

Men were hunters and warriors. Women were gatherers and shamans who gave visions to the people to guide them. Women were not inferior to men in all realms of life, and they possessed the significant authority of their own, which was frequently centered on their matrilineal lineage, or "girdle group": women of the same matrilineal heritage wore a kut, a narrow girdle of known weaving unique to that group. Because men were barred from seeing or even discussing the girdles, a woman's daughters-in-law could not be of the same girdle group; it was the women who controlled Ainu's fertility. In Ainu mythology, women are often shown as powerful, even warlike. They battle alongside their male counterparts and are perfectly capable of repelling intruders or completing daily duties like hunting and fishing on their own.

Grasp Ainu religion requires an understanding of two concepts: Ramat and Kamui. All living things, both plants and animals, and objects, particularly those related to humanity, possess the immanent power of Ramat.

Ramat is a nonsentient force that can possess a whole and functional item and then depart it when it is destroyed or dies. In this way, Ramat resembles Polynesian mana and, predictably, Japanese kami. The Ramat leaves a thing when it is destroyed, just as it does when a person dies. Humans, as larger and more sophisticated organisms, have more ramat than simple devices and beings like tools or seeds.

Ainu religion's deities are known as Kamui. They are divided into various subclasses, some of which are more powerful than others. There is a significant distinction between pirika Kamui (good Kamui), wen Kamui (hostile, malevolent), and koshne Kamui (hostile, malevolent) (neutral). Again, there are striking parallels between Ainu and Japanese concepts, indicating that they either share a common ancestor or have been influencing one another for a long time. The Kamui are human-like in appearance. They live, love, and even die like humans. However, once they leave their habitat and visit the Ainu homeland, they are or can be, exceedingly powerful. The Kamui and Ainu share a mutually beneficial connection. Offerings to the Kamui were central to Ainu's religious practice. Wine, food, and valuable things are among the offerings, with inau being the most important.

Every Kamui has an inau that is unique to that deity. Humans are the only ones who can make inau. The craftsman would skillfully shave curling sections from a thick wand of willow or other trees. These were molded into shapes appropriate to the Kamui in issue while still attached to the tip of the wand. The inau were Kamui in and of themselves, albeit their sole purpose was to transmit the respect and gifts of the maker. Inau would be buried in appropriate locations—before the fire, by a riverbank, at the bedside of a sick person—and offerings of food, drink, singing, and dancing would be offered there. Kamui is very reliant on offerings and inau, as we can see from the Yukari poems. The particular Kamui's power will decrease without the food, wine, and other offerings, and he or she may finally become moribund. Without the inau to deliver the gift, either the Kamui recipient will not receive it or will not know who is responsible for it if they do.

The Kamui could take on any form, and in exchange for human contributions, they would "dress" in animal, tree, or vegetable "clothes." The outer garments of a Kamui were a fish or a whale, a tree, or an animal, which were given to the Ainu when the deity returned to the Kamui homeland. The Kamui shed these outer robes and gave them to the person who was being visited. The deity's Ramat was still attached to the artifact, which had to be treated with reverence. The Kamui would provide a gift to a hunter who caught a fine game or a gatherer who discovered delicious lily bulbs.

The bear ritual, which was practiced until the early twentieth century, exemplified this practice. A year was spent raising a baby bear cub before it was murdered with arrows. The meat and fur were eventually eaten, but the bear was shown for a week and given wine and amusement before being returned to his homeland without his "clothing": the empty husk of the bear cub's body, which he left behind as a gift to his hosts. Bears were particularly significant to the Ainu in general. Bears were generally considered kind and well-disposed toward humans in their experience (the Asian brown bear Ursus arctos, of which the Hokkaido brown bear is a subspecies, is related to the American grizzly). They were, in effect, the outer clothes worn by the mountain god Nuparikor Kamui when he came to see humans, seeking offerings of wine and inau and leaving his earthly husk or covering—the bear's fur, meat, and bones—for the humans to enjoy. Ararush—monster bears—also appeared, mainly as a result of people failing to perform suitable rites and offerings for the bears. Ararush were feared because they not only did not graciously surrender their clothing to the hunters, but they also stalked and attacked people, dammed rivers to preserve the salmon themselves, and scared deer and other food animals away.

There were four realms in Ainu cosmology. People lived in two of them: the realm of the land, or land mass (Hokkaido), and the realm of the sea islands beyond the horizon, with the Ainu in one and their enemies—Japanese and Okhotskians—in the other. The Kamui lived in their own realm, which was quite similar to that of humans in every manner, and was frequently depicted as being high in the sky. The fourth realm was the dark and ominous domain of individuals who had acted badly in life. Such miserable souls, whether human or Kamui, were doomed to wander that damp and dismal land, whereas those who acted appropriately, reciprocating hospitality and performing rituals, were held in the hearth by the Hearth Goddess until reincarnated.

Chapter 4-Sources of Japanese Mythology

We seek data about Japanese mythology from two different types of sources. Textual canons exist in both Shinto and Buddhism, from which myths have been derived. Few of these written books have the same stature as the Christian Bible in terms of unquestionable truth. Nonetheless, they, like the Bible, contain deity and hero narratives, as well as moral precepts, ritual obligations, and world explanations.

Ethnographers who have documented oral myths, generally those of the Little Traditions, are a second source. Japanese ethnographers have been vigilant in recording the myths and folktales, rites, and traditions of far-flung, often desolate communities since Yanagida (also Yanagita) Kunio and Origuchi Shinobu. Kindaichi Kysuke and Chiri Mashiho, for example, did the same for the Ainu.

4.1 The Shinto Canon

The most important texts on Shinto mythology are collections of claimed histories written during the Heian period. The Kojiki (Record of Ancient Matters, compiled approximately 712 C.E.) and Nihonshoki (Record of Ancient Matters, compiled circa 712 C.E.) are two of the most important (Chronicles of Japan, compiled circa 720 C.E., often referred to as Nihongi). Both offer legendary (or at least unverifiable) and historical narratives of Japan's history, from mythical times until the reign of the first emperors.

Neither work was viewed in particularly high respect until the eighteenth century (Nihonshoki slightly more than Kojiki). However, in the mid-eighteenth century, Motoori Norinaga, a

Kokugaku (National Learning) scholar, began work on his huge (49 books) Kojiki-den—a commentary on the Kojiki. The old Japanese stories, he believed, represented the people's charter history, free of Confucian or Buddhist influences. The elevation of the Kojiki, and with it, the Nihonshoki, is thus obviously linked to political ideals connected with the Tokugawa shogunate's fall.

Both works have a similar tone and cover a lot of the same ground in slightly different ways. The Nihonshoki, on the other hand, has a variety of alternate versions of mythology, such as "Some say this, others say that..." The Nihonshoki likewise has a more Chinese influence, borrowing Chinese vocabulary and explanations, whereas the Kojiki is more self-consciously Japanese. Both volumes are made up of short chapters, with the first recounting the actions of the gods and the second describing occurrences during the reigns of specific emperors. The Nihonshoki has a modest focus on the latter and also covers events related to the advent of Buddhism, which the Kojiki ignores. There are a few other compilations of lower reputation and importance. The Engishiki, for example, is a collection of norito (declamatory prayers). The Fudoki, a collection of local stories, records of customs, and gazetteers from various parts of Japan gathered during the Heian period, is another example. Many of them are simply scraps, while only minor portions of others have been translated into English.

In a variety of styles, the sources of heroic and subsequent myths have been recorded or mentioned. Japanese mythology can be found in song-recitation texts, plays, and novels, albeit they frequently contradict one another. Some, but far from all, of this literature, has been translated into languages other than Japanese, such as the Heike Monogatari (Tale of the Heike).

Another valuable resource is the graphic arts. Japanese painting and sculpture, as well as lacquer and enameling arts, frequently depict mythological topics. Buddhist sages, heroes, and deities are frequently duplicated and depicted in art, sometimes with prose or poetic remarks.

These depictions are crucial for understanding how the Japanese thought about mythical events and figures during specific periods. People still construct Daruma dolls to assure effort, and they still offer the gigantic Ni-o straw shoes for their bare feet since depictions of Daruma (the fabled founder of Zen) and the Ni-o temple guardians are still "mythicized" by people today.

4.2 Buddhist Literature: The Sutras and Commentaries

Buddhism has a large body of literature. An attempt was undertaken soon after Shakyamuni's death to write down what he had spoken during his forty-five years of preaching. Even back then, there were differences, with some followers effectively contending, "Yes, you are correct, the Buddha most likely said such and such at a specific occasion, but he taught me something different under different conditions."

A hundred years later, a second pan-Buddhist conference contributed more material, but it did not decrease disagreements or produce a unified canon of work or any statement similar to the basics documented for Christianity in the Nicene confession. As the Buddha's followers traveled over East and Central Asia, they continued to write books, attempting to explain or settle issues that they believed were important. They also came into contact with other ideologies, such as Persia's Zoroastrianism, Tibet's Bon, and even Christianity, and attempted to interpret the Buddha's teachings in light of what they learned.

The core Buddhist writings are divided into sutras (Sanskrit for "thread"). These sutras were either quick expositions of Buddhist teaching or comprehensive essays on the subject, including Shakyamuni's preaching. In Japan, two sutras are particularly important: the Diamond Sutra and the Lotus Sutra. Most Japanese Buddhist interpretations place one or the other at the center of their beliefs. The issue, in our opinion, is that the mythological personalities mentioned are frequently just addressed in passing in these works.

Other literature, such as exegesis from Hindu, Chinese, Tibetan, and no longer extant Central Asian manuscripts, are the resources from which much of Japanese Buddhist mythology is built. The Daizo Kyo (Collected Buddhist writings) contains a more or less agreed-upon canon of books, albeit it only covers a portion of what can be termed Buddhist source works. Many of these works were adapted from works that have since gone or had limited general appeal but drew the attention of a scholar or clergyman.

Japanese Buddhist mythology also includes folktales and morality tales about or told by Buddhist miracles and miracle workers. These stories, many of which have been collected into compilations such as the Konjaku Monogatari (but only a few of which have been translated from Japanese), provide a rich source of beliefs about deities and Buddhas, as well as myths about their powers.

4.3 Ainu Yukari

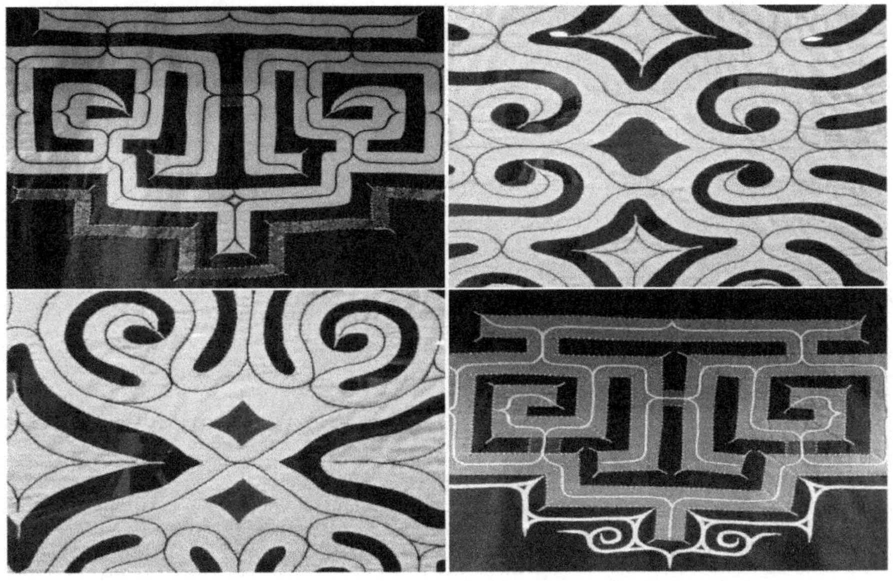

The Ainu had no written language of their own. They did, maybe, as a result, manage to preserve a large oral poetry tradition that was presented publicly. Much of Ainu mythology was preserved in Kamui yukar, or "deity epics," in which a singer told a deity's story in verse. These epics, some of which were over 7,000 verses long, were sung at assemblies by a singer who assumed the role of the Kamui (culture hero). A person who could recite a poem in its entirety was highly regarded. The deities and heroes were the subjects of this poetry, which were passed down from father to son and mother to daughter. When time and other activities were allowed, they were repeated in formal gatherings and used as entertainment. Western missionaries and Japanese ethnographers (and subsequently some Ainu trained in those sciences) began recording this poetry, known as Yukari, in the late nineteenth and early twentieth century with the goal of preserving them. The Ainu's significant interest in their own religious activities, as well as the practice of memorizing the Yukari, has ensured that a large number of them have survived.

This means that much of the poetry that has survived has been filtered through non-Ainu perspectives. Despite this, we gain a sense of the fundamental concerns of Ainu's life: the environment, social ties, and family issues.

Yukari is commonly divided into three categories: deity Yukari, hero Yukari, and human Yukari, and they all tell the same story. They are usually long sagas about the lives and actions of mortals and gods, narrated in the first person. Yukari occasionally contradicts one another, assigning various actors to the same events or describing the same character in different ways. In the oral literature of a culture structured into small, relatively isolated bands, this is unsurprising.

4.4 Ryukyuan Myths

As previously said, the Ryukyuans are possibly the least myth-inclined people on the planet. Few Ryukyuans, including various types of ritual professionals, are interested in discussing origin myths or deities or in debating metaphysical matters in any form. As previously mentioned, several origin stories have been collected on some of the islands, which are comparable to origin myths found elsewhere, both to the south (Taiwan and the Philippines) and to the north (Canada) (Japan).

Occasionally, fragments of the story are preserved in various works, but there is no "body" of Ryukyuan mythology akin to Japanese or Ainu myths.

The sources themselves are conflicting and even questionable, making Ryukyuan mythology difficult to classify. There are two types of sources available. A number of ethnographers and anthropologists (including Norbeck, Ouwehand, Sered, and Robinson, as well as a huge number of Japanese researchers who have not been translated into Western languages) have examined the Ryukyus' religion firsthand. The study has been constrained in most cases because it has focused on one of the small island settlements, limiting the degree of generalization feasible. These studies, on the other hand, have offered firsthand information from the people involved.

Written documents are the second source of information, with three being the most important. Between 1531 and 1623, Omoro Soshi was collected. The Omoro Soshi was a collection of poetry and literature with legendary overtones. The Okinawan monarchy had become a subordinate state of the Satsuma lords of southern Kyushu by 1609, and this collection reflects Japanese concerns.

The same can be said of the second source. The Ryukyu Shindo-ki was written by Taichu-Shonin, a Buddhist monk, in 1638. This represented his Buddhist viewpoint, which attempted to draw similarities between his Japanese Buddhist concerns and his missionary work on Okinawa. Finally, a politician and scholar named Tomohide Haneji penned Chuzan Seikan, a compendium comparable to Taichu's but more thorough.

Chapter 5-The Magic of Mythology

Traditions are a big part of what makes a culture distinct. By word of mouth, writing, or example, a culture's customs of eating, speaking, clothing, and commemorating holidays are carried down from generation to generation. These traditions may alter throughout time as technology progresses or civilizations become more impacted by one another, but distinguishing patterns in a people's traditional behavior can still be seen.

One of the most significant aspects of traditional culture is storytelling. These tales can feature heroes or villains, creation or destruction, huge battles won or lost, epic voyages, or child or animal adventures. A myth is a unique type of story.

5.1 Myths, Legends, Folktales, and Fairy Tales

People can usually identify the difference between factual stories and stories that the storyteller and the audience are aware are being given for entertainment; however, this is not always the case. Even if the stories aren't genuine, they nevertheless convey ideals. We don't believe fairy tales like Cinderella are factual, but we do know that Cinderella's behavior is superior to her sisters'—especially in the German version, in which Cinderella's sisters' eyes are pecked out by small birds. Fairy stories, like legends and myths, provide insight into our feelings about ourselves, others, and the world around us.

Myths are a type of story that was initially handed down orally by word of mouth. The distinction between a myth and a folktale, according to traditional story scholars, is that a myth is told as factual. Myths are stories that individuals believe or are told to believe by the people in their culture. A myth, unlike a tale, such as those about Johnny Appleseed or Paul Bunyan, may be set in ancient history, before the world as we know it existed. Information concerning gods or supernatural entities, as well as interactions between gods and humans, may be found in myths. Myths frequently explain how everything came to be the way they are now and provide answers to questions regarding the origins of the universe and life, such as: Where did the world come from? How did the sun and moon first appear in the sky? Why is it necessary for individuals to die? After we die, what happens to us? What is the difference between men and women? Cosmologies, or cosmogonies, are myths that explain how the universe is structured, how it began, and, typically, where humans fit into the grand scheme of things. They are derived from the Greek term kosmos, which means "order." Myths instruct people on how to treat a deity or gods, as well as one another. They clarify why people observe particular festivals or do certain rituals (traditional activities or ceremonies like those associated with birth, marriage, becoming an adult, and death). Myths frequently deal with enigmatic and incomprehensible subjects. They are often sacrosanct and tied to a culture's religion; however, this is not always the case.

Heroes who are part human and part divine are also depicted in myths. Following the arrival of Buddhism, some Japanese tales talk of famous Zen masters, warriors, or monks. They, like the Buddha, are historical persons who transform into supernatural beings, which isn't a problem in a culture where people become gods after death.

5.2 Interpreting Mythology Through the Ages

If "falsehood" comes to mind when you hear the word "myth," you might be interested to discover that the Greek philosopher Plato uttered it first. Plato contrasted rational reasoning with legendary imagination in the early fourth century BCE. Plato considered mythology to be the polar opposite of reason. Plato and the ancient Greeks gave us the concept of a myth, which is an inaccurate interpretation of a scientific or historical occurrence. The contemporary scientific approach and the manner of looking at and analyzing evidence were paved by the thought of Greek philosophers. It did not, however, put an end to myth or religion or even prevent myths from growing, as Christianity and Islam established world religions after Plato, but it did provide a new manner of raising and answering questions concerning the world's creation.

The conflict between these two ways of looking at the world has lingered throughout history. During the Age of Enlightenment, in the seventeenth and eighteenth centuries, scientific intellectuals once again rejected myths. Enlightenment thinkers argued that mythology obstructs honest research. They pondered why people believed such stuff. After studying the newly "found" (and vanquished) peoples of the New World, historians theorized that mythology reflected a universal "childhood of man," in which nations invented stories to explain things they couldn't understand otherwise.

5.3 Why Do Myths from Different Cultures Sound the Same?

Scholars examining myths from diverse civilizations in the 18th and 19th centuries began to question why stories shared so many similarities despite the nations' differences. Did all the myths start in one place and then spread across the globe as different tribes migrated and merged? India has been mentioned as a likely location for the origins of world mythology.

Scholars interested in the origins of language attempted to explain the parallels between numerous European and Near Eastern languages at the time. The researchers traced the languages' origins to an older Indian language and then chronicled how they evolved. The similarities between mythology, according to some scholars, are due to the spread of cultures. This is correct in some cases. Because societies exchanged stories, certain Asian myths are similar to one another.

Sigmund Freud, a psychiatrist, proposed another explanation for mythological connections in the twentieth century. He proposed that myths (and dreams) embody the fundamental components of human experience in symbols. Aggression and love, according to Freud, are the most fundamental energies in human nature. Tales, according to Freud and his disciple Carl Jung, were not relics from "man's childhood," and the similarities across myths were not attributable to their spreading from a single source. Myths, according to Freud, are crucial and necessary manifestations of essential aspects of the human mind and experience.

5.4 A Mutual Human Experience

Myths are viewed by anthropologists and folklorists—social scientists who research civilizations and their traditions—as a representation of the culture in which they are transmitted. What do the specific stories of these occurrences tell us about the culture if, as it appears, most societies have had to credit for the origins of the world and the status of human beings in that creation? What do the myths have to say about the people? In what ways do myths instruct people on what they should value and how they should live? This method inquires about the contrasts as well as the commonalities across mythology. Humans are born, grow up, age, and die; we love and loathe our family; we watch the sunrise in the morning and marvel at the expanse of the night sky. Cultures, on the other hand, celebrate and mourn in various ways. They are divided on whether evil is inherent in human nature or whether people are fundamentally good. They place a greater emphasis on the individual than on the collective, or vice versa. They see gods, people, and animals as distinct entities with a definite order between them, or they see a universe where gods live in every rock and mouse. One method to look at these distinctions is to investigate a culture's myths. We can try to comprehend how other individuals see the world by doing so.

Chapter 6-The Japanese Religion

The Japanese told stories about the kami before they had written, possibly around 300 BCE.

The kami are not gods in the same sense that Zeus is. Kami isn't always cut off from the rest of the world or from people.

Kami, as per a scholar named Motoori Norinaga, are the deities of earth and heaven, as well as spirits venerated at shrines. They can also be humans, plants and trees, birds and beasts, mountains and oceans with amazing power and should be revered

Honoring the kami was not a part of organized religion in ancient times. Japan was an archipelago of islands with no centralized authority. Clans, tribes, and extended families formed the social structure. People worked the land, grew rice, and paid homage to the kami in shrines and at home. Many of the kami was probably only known to the family who revered them or to the residents of a single town. "According to one of the old Japanese chronicles," "In their world, countless spirits twinkled like fireflies, and every tree and bush spoke. "We know that the Japanese people told stories and established shrines to important kami about the third or fourth century C.E.

The shrine of Amaterasu, the sun deity, is one of them. She, like the kami of the moon and storm and others—the "Kamis of the heavenly plain"—reminds me more of the Roman or Aztec gods. They are extremely powerful beings who are not of this world and are immortal. The Sacred Mirror, which plays a crucial role in an Amaterasu story, is housed in a temple in Ise.

As previously said, Japanese mythology is made up of a variety of cultural traditions. The blended and often intermingled religious components of Shinto and Buddhism are the two primary influences. The two "outrider" cultures of the Japanese islands, the Ainu in the north and the Ryukyuans in the south, must be added to this. We'll focus on Shinto and Buddhism as religious traditions because they're the foundation for a lot of Japanese mythology.

6.1 Shinto

Shinto, Japan's native religion, did not receive its name until the Japanese felt compelled to separate their local rites from those of the imported Bukkyo or Butsu-do (Buddhism). The reverence and appeal to local spirits who dwelt in material items, usually natural or peri-natural, were central to the local religion. Mountains, strange trees, waterfalls, water, oddly formed rocks, and other items were thought to have the ability to willfully influence people's life (kami). The spirits of the dead were similar, albeit they were thought to reside in a gloomy and fetid realm, similar to the classical Greek notion of hell. Kami could and did take up residence in anything that evoked awe or merely piqued her interest. Trees, rocks, streams, and weirdly shaped stones are still considered kami in Japan today. This is in addition to the mountains, sun, and other significant geographical and natural elements.

The local religion placed a strong emphasis on personal cleansing, as well as direct interaction with the kami and the giving of gifts. Between the ordinary and kami realms, there was no obvious distinction.

Much of this has been preserved in Japan's many Little Traditions. Indigenous beliefs were culturally specific and unwritten. There was no practical limit to the number of kami that may be summoned. Some kami, such as the rice-field kami and the water kami, became specialized.

As the Yamato state grew larger and stronger, it was forced to concentrate and control its people, resorting to religion, among other things, as many states did. Local kami, their stories and rites, were therefore absorbed into or altered to fit with the imperial Great Tradition, and the Yamato state's local cult became the predominant religious system in the Japanese islands. As a result, there are two features that are somewhat contradicting. On the one hand, a collection of "fabricated" tales originating from endeavors to combine various traditions became "mainstream" Japanese mythology, especially once they were written down. These are the written mythologies issued in such Japanese states, often combining local beliefs and invariably featuring contradictions.

The tales of the Little Traditions, on the other hand, lie beneath these Great Tradition myths, fitting more or less seamlessly into the Great Tradition's underlying structure. Saints and goblins, kami and demons from local mythology all had to adapt to the prevailing viewpoint, whether they liked it or not: they were and are all kami in some way.

Only after it became necessary to separate it from Buddhism, which was brought to Japan from Korea in 522 CE, did the practice of honoring the kami become known as Shinto—which simply means "the way of the kami." The kami's stories were written down as well as passed down by word of mouth by this time, thanks to the introduction of writing from China. However, the earliest Shinto story text we have is from 712 CE. It's called Kojiki, or "Record of Ancient Matters," and it was written at the emperor's request. It contains tales regarding the formation of the globe and the Japanese islands, the origins of the sun and moon, and the beginnings of death. The Kojiki also describes the importance of ritual cleanliness and washing, both of which are fundamental to Shinto and Japanese culture.

Shinto is a religion that focuses on our everyday lives.

Although it had heaven (the High Plain of Heaven, from which the primordial gods originated) and an underworld (the Dark Land, an unclean location), its mythology had nothing in common with Christian heaven or hell. Neither is it a location where individuals go after death to be punished or rewarded. There are no commandments or explicit instructions for living in the Kojiki. It doesn't even require that people must believe in the kami; it simply tells stories about them. The Kojiki also has a god's genealogy (family tree), which claims that the emperor's line is descended from the sun kami. (The order to write the Kojiki was given to enhance the imperial family's claim to rule at a period when Buddhism and other Chinese influences were gaining traction and the numerous tribes were still not completely under the emperor's control.) The book was supposed to prove that the emperor wasn't just any kami but rather a descendant of the most powerful kami.)

Shinto, unlike many other religions, was not founded on the belief in a holy book or the acceptance of certain stories or doctrines. Shinto did not emerge from the beliefs or experiences of a single person. The spiritual ceremonies of washing and purification, as well as offerings to the kami, such as food or tokens purchased at shrines, are at the heart of Shinto. A prayer or a request is generally accompanied by these tokens. Shinto has its origins in communal and family celebrations of the yearly spring planting and fall harvest, as well as births and marriages. Shinto honors and focuses on nature since the kami are everywhere, in everything.

Because each kami has the ability to be creative or destructive, kind or aggressive, this concept of paying attention to nature is crucial.

The ceremonies assist individuals in avoiding the kami's destructive and furious tendencies. They also assist people in avoiding their aggressive and destructive sides. In Japanese mythology, a constant battle between good and evil makes little sense. Even so, humans make mistakes from time to time, and they must acknowledge and correct their errors.

6.2 The Shinto Pantheon

It is a collection of Shinto gods and goddesses.

Although there are many different types of kami, a few of them are particularly important in Shinto mythology.

IZANAGI AND IZANAMI, the original gods who created the world and countless other gods, are the main deities of the Shinto pantheon.

AMATERASU, the sun goddess and ruler of heaven, whose grandson, according to legend, became Japan's first emperor.

TSUKI-YOMI, the god of the Moon and Amaterasu's brother.

SUSANO-WO, the storm god and Amaterasu's brother. He was expelled from heaven due to a quarrel with his sister.

NINIGI-NO-MIKOTO, Amaterasu's grandson, was tasked with ruling the world.

6.3 Shinto Myths

Before they were written down, people had been telling some of this Shinto mythology for generations. They were written down for the emperor, at his direction, in the Kojiki, during a time when Japan was pondering its ties with Chinese and Korean cultures. The Shinto stories in the Kojiki are official accounts meant to show the emperor's divinity, among other things.

However, there were many recorded and oral versions of these myths before that. The Katari-be, or "corporations of reciters," existed even before writing, but they became less prominent after the stories were written down. Many variations of the mythology existed, as is typically the case. There wasn't necessarily one that was "correct."

6.4 Kami

Kami is at the center of early Japanese religious activities. The word is commonly rendered as "gods" or "deities" in English, but the notion is much more intricate.

Kami can be classified into two groups. The first is about natural occurrences. A mountain or a stream, for example, may be regarded to be home to a kami. During the growing season, a mountain kami may be spotted assisting a farmer by delivering water. Although this spirit or energy may not always support humans, its favor can be advantageous to them. The inverse is also true: an enraged kami can wreak havoc.

The ancestor spirits, also known as Uji-kami or clan deities, are the second type of kami. These spirits may be able to assist people in the present. They do, however, do a lot more than that. Honoring one's ancestors helps to bring together the wider family that descended from them. The clan and society as a whole benefit from maintaining these relationships. These spirits hold a person accountable for his or her actions. When a person does something dishonorable, the ancestors are also disgraced.

The kami structure mirrored society's organization, with leaders or kings at the top and "ordinary people" at the bottom. The more powerful kami may be able to assist an entire village or region.

There is no such thing as an all-powerful or faultless kami. In Japanese mythology, the ujikami (ujigami) frequently perform things that humans would do, such as getting into difficulty or offending people. They resemble Greek or Roman gods in this way.

Shrines to the kami, as well as most prayers and rituals addressing them, were not very ornate in early Japan. Local government officials were also responsible for maintaining shrines and performing rituals commemorating prominent clan ancestors. As a result, religion and government were entwined in the social fabric.

Certain members of the clan were entitled or allowed to keep ancestral kami shrines. Anyone, however, might pray to a kami, whether it was an ancestor god or one associated with a natural occurrence.

Early Shinto rites included shamans, who could speak with kami and employ supernatural power to heal humans.

Women made up the majority of these shamans. The function of the shaman was passed down through the generations in some households. For contacting the dead and summoning the gods, they had particular processes and ceremonies.

According to ancient Japanese history, there are approximately eight million kami. There are more kami than anyone can count, even though the quantity was not meant literally. Every hamlet had its own specific deity forces and spirits that guarded it. Every family honored their forefathers and mothers. And telling stories or myths about people who had gone before was a vital method for families to remember the past while also demonstrating their place in the present.

6.5. Buddhism

In the 5th and 6th centuries B.C., India was the birthplace of Buddhism.

The religion, which was founded by Siddhartha Gautama, the Buddha, or "Enlightened One" (known in Japan as SHAKA), acknowledged that being human implies suffering. To be free of pain, one must give up wants and walk the EIGHTFOLD Moral path. The Buddhist must think, act, determine, speak, act, strive, converse, and focus in accordance with these eight precepts. A soul can only reach Nirvana, or ENLIGHTENMENT, by doing so. Different people define enlightenment in different ways. It might be viewed as a way out of the never-ending cycle of REBIRTH or as an infinite state of happiness and tranquility.

Buddhism flourished throughout Asia, eventually reaching China in the first century A.D. By the sixth century, it had made its way from China to Korea and eventually Japan.

When the Korean monarch handed the Japanese emperor a golden statue of the Buddha in the sixth century C.E., Buddhism was introduced to Japan. By this time, Buddhism had been around for 1,000 years and had assumed several forms in different parts of the world.

Unlike Shinto, a Japanese religion with no founder or theology, Buddhism had priests, a large number of written scriptures, and well-defined beliefs. The notion that people are intended to learn enlightenment and eventually escape themselves from the cycle of reincarnation—death and rebirth—and a physical world of pain is at the heart of these beliefs.

There were many different sects or forms of Buddhism during the period. The sects highlighted various teachings from and about BUDDHA. They gradually developed opposing viewpoints on the nature of the cosmos and how enlightenment may be attained.

While they shared many beliefs, the sects were divided by their disagreements.

The principles of a school known as MAHAYANA, or "Greater Vehicle" or "Greater Vessel," BUDDHISM became the most influential kind of Buddhism in Japan. The innate Buddha is present in all animals, according to one of this school's major doctrines. Enlightenment can be attained if a person can connect with that innate character. However, for most of us, doing so without assistance is difficult, if not impossible.

Mahayana Buddhists consider that the historical Buddha was just one incarnation of the eternal Buddha or life power. There have been many Buddhas, and there is constantly one Buddha in the universe, according to Mahayana Buddhism. These mighty beings have many "elements," or attributes, that highlight different aspect of the perpetual Buddha.

In addition, there are a number of BODHISATTVAS, or Buddhas-to-be (BOSATSU in Japanese), who can assist people in achieving enlightenment.

Rather than the Korean version of Buddhism, Chinese Buddhism was eventually adopted by the Japanese court and then by the general public. Chinese Buddhism, on the other hand, was absorbed and altered rather than being replaced by Shinto, as Japanese society adapts and reinterprets all it learns from foreign cultures. If we consider culture to be a rich soup, the introduction of Chinese Buddhism to Japan was not like adding noodles, which are separate from the broth, but rather like adding an ingredient that becomes a part of the broth itself. This fusion of Shinto and Buddhism has persisted to this day.

Buddhism introduced the concept of an afterlife to the Japanese religion, describing a time when people were evaluated, then rewarded or punished. The distinctions between Buddhism and Shinto are frequently muddled. Ryobu-Shinto, or "Double-Shinto," refers to the blending of Buddhist and Shinto doctrines.

Buddhism preaches personal redemption and freedom from the cycle of birth, death, and rebirth, although it has many different branches. It used to teach that people had to follow the teachings of the Buddha, who was the founder of the religion and later became the subject of many tales. Another branch said that individuals might seek assistance from a plethora of minor gods, who are more akin to saints or kami in Japan, which embraced this version of Buddhism.

There are also a variety of Buddhist gods and other beings who can be invoked. These collectively represent a wide range of mythological figures. Their origin is complex, but the majority of them can take on human or near-human forms.

Because a Buddhist god might take on many various forms, it seemed only reasonable to propose that certain kami were simply Buddhas or bosatsu in disguise.

6.6 The Merging of Buddhism and Shinto

The Buddhist monk Kobo DAISHI is credited with developing the doctrine that enables the two religions to work together. RYOBU-SHINTO, or "Shinto with two faces," was his theory. It was conceivable to link Shinto gods with entities from Buddhist mythology using this approach. Amaterasu, for example, may be considered the Japanese equivalent of Vairocana, whose name means "sunlike." Vairocana is the perpetual Buddha's all-powerful, sunlike incarnation. In this way, the most significant Shinto god was considered a counterpart of the Buddhist pantheon's most essential member.

The TENDAI branch of Buddhism came up with a similar concept. SANNO SHINTO was the name of the philosophy. The global Buddha is the central and most significant figure in Tendai Buddhism. Tendai devotees, on the other hand, realize that Buddha uses a variety of vehicles to help people gain enlightenment, including minor gods, scriptures, and stories, as taught in the Lotus Sutra. In Buddhism and Shinto, this philosophy supported syncretism or the mixing of diverse beliefs. It prompted devotees to explore analogies and establish links between many gods and traditions.

The embrace of Buddhism by the SOGA clan, a powerful family at the imperial court, aided the religion's acceptance, yet many fires and other disasters were blamed on Buddhist gods intruding into locations holy to the Shinto kami. Finally, Shinto priests from the USA shrine, devoted to HACHIMAN, took part in a ritual in the mid-eighth century to extend the kami's protection to a Buddhist temple built in Nara. Other kami was summoned soon after to defend other TEMPLES.

Buddhists reciprocated the gesture. Hachiman, a Japanese mythic character, was designated as a Buddhist mythic figure or bosatsu. Buddhist teachers established the belief that kami were uninformed as Buddhist influence grew. As a result, Buddhist influence was required to assist them in achieving enlightenment. To ease the process, a temple was constructed near Shinto shrines. During the Yamato period, Shinto shrines were increasingly elaborate. The combined shrine temples were even more impressive.

Priests and other specialists may create clear borders between the many gods. The two systems, however, tended to mix in most people's minds. Both kami and Buddhist figures can be honored. Being a Buddhist didn't imply abandoning Shinto.

6.7 The Buddhist Pantheon

Zen Buddhism was founded by Bodhi Dharma, an Indian monk who journeyed to China. He fell asleep one day while practicing meditation. He was so enraged with himself when he awoke that he severed his eyelids, assuring that he would never sleep again. The first tea plants sprouted from his eyelashes. Tea is considered sacred by Zen Buddhists, yet it contains enough caffeine to keep people awake. Despite the fact that Bodhi Dharma is thought to be a historical figure, the tale is similar to the Shinto myth in which the body parts of a severed god are converted into delicacies that are vital to civilization.

In Japan, there are three Buddhist deities: Amida, Kannon, and Jizo, all of whom are regarded as gods of mercy. (There are numerous other gods as well, though they are less well-known.)

From China, the first god, Amida (Buddha), was passed down to Japanese culture. Because India is the birthplace of Buddhism, it is derived from the Sanskrit figure Amitabha. Amida is a bodhisattva ("enlightened being") who waited for all mankind to be redeemed before seeking salvation for himself.

Kannon, the second god of kindness, is a bodhisattva whose desire to protect humanity manifests as delayed salvation.

He is a God who guards children (and women during childbirth). Kannon is revered among Japanese Buddhists for his wisdom and counsel. Senju Kannon, or the "Kannon of a Thousand Arms," is the most common depiction of Kannon. These photos resemble those of Indian bodhisattvas, who are depicted with all of their arms spread in a compassionate attitude. Senju Kannon is frequently seen in Japan with a small Amida on his head. Kannon is sometimes represented as a horse-headed figure with a third eye or as a lotus-holding figure. Jizo is the Buddhist god of mercy's third manifestation. He, like Kannon, guards children, particularly those who have died. Jizo also guards the spirits of those who are suffering. Buddhists in Japan believe that Jizo can save tormented souls from damnation. In Japan, there are many temples dedicated to Jizo.

It's difficult to create a statement about the entire Buddhist pantheon, or collection of holy creatures, that is both complete and acceptable to all sects and practices. However, for the sake of this book, these beings can be divided into three categories: Buddhas, Bosatsu, and Kings or Guardians.

"Buddha" simply means "one who has attained enlightenment" in its most basic definition. All Buddhists believe that Buddhism's founder attained enlightenment. Most people also believe that others have done the same. AMIDA, a major deity for the PURE LAND sects, is Japan's most important Buddha. Saying his name after death, according to believers, put the soul in the Pure Land, where enlightenment was attainable.

Bosatsu, or "future Buddhas," are spirits that have completed their preparations for enlightenment but have chosen to postpone it in order to serve others. (It's worth noting that bosatsu's enlightenment is already guaranteed.) The most prominent bosatsu in Japan were FUDO, a version of the Indian god Shiva, KANNON, the bosatsu of empathy, and FUGEN, the bosatsu of rationality, according to experts.

Last but not least, there are "fierce Buddhas," as well as monarchs and guardians, in the Buddhist pantheon. The Buddhas' ferocious Buddhas fight for them. East, West, north, south, and center are the five-compass points of heaven. These are known in Japan as MYO-O, and depictions of them can commonly be found guarding Buddhist temples and monasteries. The temple entrances and shrines are also guarded by two lesser deities known as NIO or GUARDIAN KINGS.

With the exception of sects in Sri Lanka, where Pattin is revered as a significant divinity, there are few female gods in the Buddhist pantheon. This is a result of gender norms at the period, which put males in a stronger position in most of the civilizations where Buddhism arose.

In a single statement, the following are the Buddhist Gods worshipped in Japan

Amida, a powerful guardian of humanity

DAINICHI NYORAI a significant Buddha who is particularly revered by the Tendai and SHINGON sects.

Fugen, the future Buddha of knowledge and insight (bosatsu)

Kannon is a bosatsu with a variety of forms.

Fudo, a Myo-o who fights avarice, rage, and foolishness.

JIZO is an extremely powerful bosatsu.

EMMA-O, the devil's god.

IDA-TEN, who keeps an eye on monasteries.

6.8 Influences from other Chinese cultures

While Buddhism was the most significant Chinese impact on Japanese mythology during the Yamato era and the years after, there were other significant Chinese repercussions on Japan during the Yamato era and the years after. Taoism and Confucianism were the most influential in terms of mythology. Confucianism is a school of ideas and ethics that has had a significant influence on Japanese society and institutions while not being a religion. During the age of rising Chinese influence in Japan, Taoism made its way to the country. The Tao, or "Way," incorporates old Chinese folk religion and beliefs with philosophy. One of Taoism's basic concepts is that one should accept the universe's method of doing things; fate is unavoidable, and one must bend to it like a young tree covered in ice during a windstorm. The notion that everything is generated by two opposing energies, or yin and yang, is also important to Taoism and Chinese thought. All reality is shaped by the juxtaposition of opposites, such as heat and cold, life and death. This concept is central to onmyo, a Taoist style of divination that arrived in Japan during this time period from China. Onmyo-ji, or wandering priests, researched omens and gave advice on when the best time to do things like getting married was.

Chapter 7-Origin Stories of Japanese Gods and Goddesses

According to the Japanese, there are more than eight million kami, or "800 myriads." This isn't supposed to be a precise figure. Since everyone and everything is a potential kami, eight million is another way of meaning countless—or perhaps limitless.

Some of the innumerable Kamis are comparable to the Greek, Roman, and Egyptian gods and goddesses. They come from a time before the contemporary world, when the kami formed and fought with one another, sent death into the world, and occasionally acted evilly, such as ruining irrigation canals and murdering kin. They also acted in ways that Japanese people were expected to act, such as washing their hands with water.

One of the things that have kept stories intriguing and perplexing for thousands of years is the gods' proclivity for awful acts.

It's sometimes good to think of the kami as a model of what not to do in Japan. Their misadventures demonstrate what they can get away with — or not — but what we, as simple humans, cannot. Their actions indicate that they do not belong in our modern environment but rather in a previous era. When a god enters the underworld and finds himself in difficulties, it instructs us to leave the underworld alone. We also learn about the culture's concept of the afterlife. It is a realm of filth and deterioration in Japanese and Shinto mythology.

7.1 The Deities of the Heavens

The first three kami appeared before there was breath or form, before heaven and earth were split, and before there were names. They were unnoticed. The earth "drifted like a jellyfish" and appeared like "floating oil." Something resembling young reeds sprang, and two more unseen kami emerged from them. They are known as the Separate Heavenly Deities and are not described since they are not seen. Other gods appeared, but they were all invisible (at least to humans). Takamagahara, or the "High Plains of Heaven," is home to these gods.

Amanominakanushi-nokami, or "Lord of the Center of Heaven," was the oldest of these gods. Takamimusubi and Kamimusubi were two additional kami of the High Plains of Heaven. The five Separate Heavenly Deities were produced by these three kami, as well as two lesser gods named Umashiashikabihikoji-no-kami and Amanotokotachi-no-kami, who were followed by seven generations of heavenly gods and goddesses.

7.2 The World Creation by Izanagi and Izanami

Izanagi-no-Mikoto ("The August—distinguished and grand—Male") and Izanami-no-Mikoto ("The August—distinguished and grand—Wife") were the last two heavenly deities created ("The August Female"). The other celestial deities gave them the heavenly jeweled spear and told them to "complete and solidify the drifting continent."

On the Heavenly Floating Bridge, Izanagi and Izanami stood (perhaps a rainbow or the Milky Way). They churned the primordial salt seas with the spear, koworo korowo ni, generating a churning sound. The seawater trickled down when they lifted the spear, forming solid land: Onogoro Island.

Izanagi and Izanami descended from the sky to build a pillar and a castle on this island. Izanagi from the left and Izanami from the right agreed to walk around the pillar. Izanami was the first to speak when they met. Then Izanagi said something. He was, however, dissatisfied. He stated that the man should be the one to talk first. They had a kid soon after, but Hiruko was a malformed creature known as a "leech child," so they put her on a reed boat and sailed her out to sea. (After the birth of a couple's first child, an old Japanese ritual involves placing a clay figurine in a small reed boat and casting it out to sea.)

Izanagi and Izanami decided to speak with the heavenly deities about what had gone wrong, and the deities conducted divination by heating a deer's shoulder blade and studying the fractures that appeared. The gods advised them that the man should have been the one to speak first. The devil child was born as a result of his mother speaking out of turn during the wooing ritual, a legend that some people feel today adds to—or reflects—inequalities between men and women in modern Japan.

After that, Izanagi and Izanami returned to the island and repeated the process, with Izanagi speaking first this time. Izanami then gave birth to Japan's eight islands. The kami, who would later dwell and rule the islands, were born after that. Wind gods, sea gods, rivers gods, tree gods, mountains gods, plains gods, seasons gods, and many others were among them.

7.3 The Death of Izanami

Izanami was scorched and got unwell while giving birth to Kagu-tsuchi, the god of fire. She vomited out the gods of metal and mining during her last struggles. She urinated on the gods of water and the aquatic green flora. She excreted, and the gods of clay or soil were found in her dung. She died after that, and Izanagi buried her.

In his anguish, Izanagi sobbed and raged. He responded, "I have given up my lovely spouse in return for a simple child." His tears gave birth to the kami known as the "Weeping Marsh Woman." In a fit of wrath, he drew his sword and slashed Kagu-head tsuchi's off. Other gods, known as the kami, "born of a sword," were created from the fire god's blood and all of his body parts. They are gods of fire and rocks, as well as the gods of volcanoes and earthquakes.

To find his wife, Izanagi traveled to the region of darkness, Yomi-tsu-Kuni, the underworld. "I found her near the gloomy gateway to the underworld, wrapped in shadows," he remarked when he found her "h, my lovely spouse, the lands are still being built. "You must return!" " She took a step back and urged Izanagi not to look her in the eyes.

It was already too late. Izanami had previously "eaten at the hearth," which meant she had had underworld fare. She did say, however, that she would ask the Yomi gods if she might return to earth and that Izanagi should not gaze at her. However, he became antsy and curious while Mom was away. It has been a long time. He broke a tooth from his comb in his hair and used it as a torch since he was desperate to see his wife again. He entered the chamber where Izanami had gone and immediately recognized her as a rotting corpse swarming with crawling maggots.

Izanagi was terrified and ran, but Izanami was furious at him for humiliating her. Yomi's hags were dispatched to pursue him. Izanagi tossed his hair vine down, and it produced grapes, which the hags stopped and ate. He yanked the comb from his hair and tossed it down when they pursued him again. It bore bamboo shoots this time. The hags came to a halt and ate once more. Izanagi bolted once more, his sword flailing behind him. He tossed three peaches at his pursuers (who by this time comprised the hags, Yomi warriors, and eight thunder gods who had formed in Izanami's body) and implored them to help him, which they did.

Izanami pursued him at the time, but he eluded her and moved a massive rock to block the pass between them. They divorced after breaking their wedding vows. Izanami pledged she would kill 1,000 people every day, whereas Izanagi swore he would give birth to 1,500 people every day, taking into account both human mortality and population growth.

Izanami was transformed into a kami of the land of death. In Shinto myth, it is a region of darkness, decay, and pollution rather than a place of retribution or judgment (in the sense of ritual uncleanliness).

7.4 The Birth of the Sun and Moon

According to Izanagi, "I've visited a dreadful, filthy land. "I need to cleanse myself." " (After a period of grieving, the Japanese continue to take a ritual bath.) Izanagi bathed at the mouth of a creek in Hyuga (northeast Kyushu), removing his garments from whence numerous Kamis were born. Other gods were born as a result of his bathing. The final three were the most crucial. Amaterasu-no-Mikoto, literally "August [important] Person Who Makes the Heavens Shine," was born when he washed his left eye. Tsuki-Yomi-no-Mikoto ("the August Moon") was born when he bathed his right eye. Susano no-Mikoto ("the August Raging Male") was born after he cleaned his nose.

Izanagi was overjoyed at the sight of these three great offspring, and he bestowed his power upon them. He decided to partition the earth and assign a portion of it to each god. "You shall reign the High Plains of Heaven," he murmured to Amaterasu, handing her a jingling necklace.

"You shall control the kingdom of the night," he said to Tsuki.

"You shall control the ocean," he stated to Susano, despite the fact that Susano is also the kami of storms that arise from the sea.

Susano sobbed and howled till mountain vegetation withered and rivers and seas dried up, and Amaterasu and Tsuki departed to rule the realms that had been entrusted to them obediently. (He appears to have depleted the world's water supply rather than adding to it, as a storm would later.) "Why do you mourn and howl instead of controlling the territory entrusted to you?" his father inquired. Susano replied, "I wish to visit my mother's homeland."

Inzaghi was furious, and he expelled Susano, stating, "You may not reside in my territory." There are two endings to this last myth. Susano ascended to heaven and is now residing in the Sun's Younger Palace. Susano is enshrined at Taga (in Shiga Prefecture, Honshu) in the other version of this narrative.

7.5 Susano Challenges His Sister

Susano stated that if he were to be exiled, he would first see his sister, Amaterasu. The mountains and rivers screamed when he arrived. The ground trembled. The sun goddess mistook this for her brother's attempt to seize her territory, and she prepared for a fight. She wore two quivers of arrows, one with 1,000 arrows and the other with 500 arrows, and tied her long hair in bunches. She stomped on the soil, plunging to her thighs and stomping the earth as if it were light snow, wearing the arm guard that shields the arm from the bow string. "What brought you here?" she inquired of her brother.

Amaterasu wasn't sure if she should believe Susano when he swore he had no bad intentions. They agreed to a competition in which each of them would have to bear children. Susano's sword was requested by Amaterasu. She chewed the pieces and spat out three goddesses after breaking them into three pieces and washing them. Susano demanded Amaterasu's hair-bead string, chewed it up and spat out a male god. The vines in her hair and the beads on her arms were treated in the same way.

Who came up on top? They couldn't agree on anything. Susano had fathered the male children, but she claimed ownership because he had utilized Amaterasu's items. He, on the other hand, claimed that the competition was meant to test his sincerity. He confirmed this by assisting in the birth of the first three "graceful maidens."

Susano then went into a triumphant rage. He covered the irrigation ditches and broke down the ridges between his sister's rice paddies. He defecated in the hall where the first fruits were consumed, scattering his excrement.

Amaterasu didn't reprimand him, possibly in the hopes of calming him down, but it didn't work. Susano then skinned a heavenly pony backward and heaved it through the roof of the heavenly weaving hall where his sister was sewing (possibly a piebald, speckled one, which is supposed to mimic the stars in many cultures). A weaving maiden was surprised to the point of injury and death.

7.6 The Sun Conceals Herself

Amaterasu was terrified, so she took refuge in the Heavenly Rock Cave, or Ama-no-iwato, a cave or rock-dwelling. The world of humans was in darkness on the High Plain of the Heavenly Deities and the Central Land of the Reed Plains. The only night was there. The kami's shouts grew louder in dread, and horrible events occurred.

Omopi-Kane-no-kami pondered the issue further. (The kami Omopo literally means "to contemplate," and she is the one who is always called upon to come up with ideas for the celestial Kamis.) His moniker implies that he is a "thought-combining-kami," or someone who can hold several thoughts or think with multiple Kamis.) The kami eventually built a big mirror and hung it from the limbs of a sacred mountain tree. A white and blue cloth was hanging in the tree. A perch with a rooster perched at the top of the tree (which took on the shape of a Shinto shrine). One kami held the tree in place while the other murmured serious magic words. Then a lovely kami named Ama-no-uzume stood on an upside-down bucket and danced, exposing her body, to the delight of the eighty countless kami. (This wasn't a nightclub act; it was the dance of a female shaman, a woman with magical abilities.)

Amaterasu slammed the door shut behind him and shouted, "The lands were supposed to be gloomy, I thought. Why are all of you smiling as Ama-no-uzume sings and dances?"

They were laughing, according to Ama-no-uzume, since a kami superior to Amaterasu had appeared. Two gods were in front of the cave door where Amaterasu was hiding, holding the mirror. It felt as if a beam of dawn had burst as she emerged and approached the mirror. Another god extended a magic rope behind her and said, "You may go no further than this!" A god who had hidden himself, a deity of enormous power, pulled her out.

As the sun rose following the darkness of her storm brother's activities, light returned to the globe. Amaterasu brought the planet back to life by restoring sunlight.

Susano was harshly punished by the eighty countless kami, who made him pay a fine of a thousand ritual offerings tables. They also took his lengthy beard, fingernails, and toenails and forcibly removed him from paradise, returning him to earth. When he returned, he got himself into additional difficulty, though he eventually slew an eight-headed dragon by getting it drunk on rice wine (sake) and chopping it up.

He found a sword that appears in much other Japanese mythology while slicing up its tail. Each new Japanese monarch is enthroned with a replica of the sword, the mirror that enticed Amaterasu from concealment, and the beads that Amaterasu wore in her hair, from which Susano created offspring. They are the three kingship symbols that connect the emperor to the gods, particularly Amaterasu, the emperor's ancestor.

7.7 Other Shinto deities

Other gods not mentioned in the previous mythology are included in the Shinto religion. "The Great Lord of the Country," Okuninushi, had eighty brothers, all of whom wanted to marry the princess Ya-gami-hime, including Okuninushi. The brothers noticed a rabbit with no fur wailing from anguish on the side of the road on their way to court the princess. The rabbit was instructed by his siblings that he needed to bathe in saline water and dry in the wind on a mountain. This, of course, made things worse for the bunny. Okuninushi instructed the rabbit to bathe in the delicious water near the river's mouth and roll in certain pollen. After being restored, the rabbit, who was actually a god, promised Okuninushi that he would marry the princess.

Okuninushi is the subject of many legends, some of which pit him against Susano, whom he eventually defeats. Okuninushi drapes his long hair to the rafters of the palace while Susano is sleeping.

Ogetsu-no-hime is a food goddess. Inari feeds either Tsukiyomi (the moon deity) or Susano in various versions of the myth. The food comes from her entire body: her mouth, nose, and even her rectum. The other god kills her because she has offended him.

Silkworms, rice, millet, red beans, wheat, and soybeans all come from her dead body—essential goods in traditional Japanese living. When this narrative about the moon god is narrated (as it is in the Nihon ON Shoki, or "Chronicles of Japan," published shortly after the Kojiki), it explains why the moon was banished to the dark sky: after his act of destruction, the sun declares that she will never see him again.

Inari, the rice god who assures a plentiful rice harvest and is also known as the god of prosperity, is one of the other gods. Ebisu is a kami who is associated with the god of labor. Kitchen appliances are even overseen by a deity in Japan! The god of cooking ranges is Kamado-no-kami. The Japanese world is teeming with kami.

7.8 Shinto Demons

Shinto, like many other world faiths, features a version of hell that was influenced by Buddhism. Jigoku is the name of the dark world, which is divided into eight areas of fire and eight regions of ice. Emma-ho is the name of Jigoku's ruler. He is in charge of evaluating the souls of male sinners and assigning them to one of the sixteen punishment areas. Female sinners are judged by his sister.

Each sinner is punished by standing in front of a mirror, which reflects his or her crimes back at him or her. Sinners' souls, on the other hand, can be saved. This salvation necessitates the assistance of a bosatsu or bodhisattva kami.

Onis are demons that can be found in both Jigoku and Earth. These demons are responsible for devastating storms, fires, disease epidemics, famines, and other natural disasters with enormous human casualties. Although some oni can take on human or animal forms, the majority remain unseen.

Chapter 8-Japanese Creatures and Spirits

The story of Japanese mythology would be incomplete if it didn't include the abundance of figures—demons and witches, goblins and ghosts—who, despite being interwoven with "holy" mythology, have no "official" existence in religious consciousness. Nonetheless, as myths or aspects of myths, these figures are essential.

These estimates are based on local people's experiences with the odd and inexplicable in their life. Some of them arose from popular Japanese interpretations of Chinese fables, whether Daoist, Buddhist, Chan (Zen) or popular in origin. They aren't organized in any way, even though such people or animals frequently appear (typically as antagonists) in the stories of the Great Tradition. They are "outlying" myths in the sense that, despite the fact that they were very real and prominent in popular mythology, they rarely had any formal existence. The elite who ruled the Great Tradition would occasionally include one or more of these aspects in the stories of the Great Tradition. These characters can be separated into human and nonhuman figures in a very broad separation; however, the line between the two is frequently blurred. Another possible division is between non-personalized beings, such as ghosts and tengu, and genuine people, such as Gama-sennin and Yuima Kji, from Japanese, Chinese, or Indian traditions.

8.1 Humans

Many of the mythological human figures are of Chinese Daoist ancestry. Philosophical Daoism, which arose with the publishing of Lao-Tao-te Tze's Ching and the Chuan-tze, was a socio-philosophical belief system in which the individual hermit was at the center. Chinese religious beliefs in ghosts and demons have always pervaded Daoism, and when these ideas were transferred to Japan, these mythological beings came along for the voyage. As a result, one character, Shki, who was rumored to be a mistreated Chinese official who had promised to combat all demons after his suicide, became well-known in Japan as a suppressor of oni (demons).

Several of these mythical figures have more of an artistic presence than in mythological discourse. However, in Japan's traditional but highly literate society, they were readily accessible to fill legendary niches when needed.

8.2 Non-humans

In Japanese mythology, there are several "tribes" of nonhuman beings. Gakki (ghosts), tengu (forest goblins), oni (demons), and kappa (demons) are the four most prevalent (water sprites). They appear as non-personalized beings or groups of creatures in most cases. They are rarely named (the Kurama tengu is an instance), yet they may be the heroes or the villains of a story.

Humanity is plagued by ghosts, a broad category of nonhumans. The emergence of Buddhism coincided with the appearance of ghosts in Japanese mythology, and they may have been a Buddhist import from China. The spirits of those who have died without being properly cared for by their family tend to manifest as ghosts. In Japan, however, certain types of ghosts were prevalent. The caring ghost, for example, is a mother who has passed away but returns to care for her newborns or children. Most ghost stories have (or have included) a Buddhist moral.

Tengu is a type of goblin who lives in the deep woods and may perform spells on the unwary (the name itself isn't correct because tengu is amoral rather than wicked). They are most afflicted by persons who do not treat them with respect. On the other hand, they are able to deliver excellent gifts to well-behaved, dedicated individuals.

In English, oni is commonly referred to as demons; however, this is also a mistake. On the one hand, oni is a misguided, wild, anti-Buddhist individual who, if they meet the appropriate person, can be turned to good. On the other side, because of their craziness, mischief, and lack of morals, they are to blame for a slew of misfortunes that strike humans. At the same time, they serve in Buddhist hells as stokers who torment the souls of sinners; a concept is taken from Buddhism and Daoism in a manner similar to some Christian ideas.

Kappa, like other types of monsters, can cause disasters, but they can also be used to learn from or obtain talents and gifts. They can also be expelled or slain, much like any nonhuman mythical figures, by people who are determined, powerful, or have the necessary spells and procedures.

Many of these creatures are "monsters," meaning they attack or threaten humans or their activities. Nonetheless, it's important to keep in mind that these creatures aren't "bad" in the traditional Western sense. They are, at best, misled, and as a result, they are paying the price for this lack of law, whether the law is viewed through the native Japanese lens of obeying higher authorities or through the Buddhist lens of observing Buddhist Law. Though it may be essential to murder such creatures on occasion, they can also be converted or subjugated by the appropriate authorities.

8.3 Shugendo

On many levels and in various ways, Shinto and Buddhism blended and melded. A succession of philosophical-religious doctrines known as Ryobu Shinto evolved in Japan throughout the Middle Ages (approximately the eleventh to sixteenth centuries).

Seishin-Ichi, the belief that the kami and Buddhist deities were one and the same, was the motivating force behind these movements. The mythological characters in both religions become more complicated as a result of this. Shugendo was a syncretic religious movement that included ascetic practices taken from both Shinto and Buddhism (fasting, bathing under waterfalls), mountain worship and pilgrimage, itinerant priests, and magical rites, among other things.

Mountain worship was an important part of many Shinto activities, and the transition to Buddhist practice was straightforward. Shugensha (Shugendo practitioner), gyoja (ascetic), yamabushi (mountain monk), or, more commonly, kebozu (hairy Buddhist priest) and bikuni (wandering nuns) would appear from the mountains, perform their magical rituals, and then vanish. This is related to the Japanese mythological concept of marebito (visiting deity).

The shugensha was particularly important because, as the only religious and medical figure many ordinary people saw in their distant hamlets, they delivered the news. That is, the shugensha and nuns (together with other roaming figures such as players and puppeteers) transported mythological ideas and stories from place to place. En no Gyoja (En the Ascetic), their patron saint, is regarded as the founder and first practitioner of the yamabushi (mountain monk; that is, ascetic) way of life.

Shugendo priests and nuns played a variety of roles, not all of which were religious or even moral. They planned and participated in pilgrimages, sold charms and medicines, and gave fortune-telling and prostitution services along the way, in addition to organizing prayer gatherings and exorcisms in remote villages and communities. Many of these activities did not endear them to the government, and they were periodically banned or suppressed throughout Japan's history. Despite this, the full set of Shugendo beliefs, which were centered on a number of distinct notable mountains, has remained to this day, albeit altered and modified. The yamabushi tradition, and more specifically, the stories told by the yamabushi and bikuni to their rural audiences as Buddhist morality tales, became one of Japan's sources of fantastic tales, legends, and myths.

Chapter 9-Mythology in Modern Japan

The myths in this book are centuries old, and neither Shinto nor Buddhism were or are essentially myth-based religions. Religion is not a very major component of the life of the Japanese, according to most reference books about modern Japan. However, Emperor Akihito, who ascended to the throne in 1989, can trace his ancestors back over 2,600 years to Emperor Jimmu and hence to the sun goddess. In October 2005, Japanese Prime Minister Junichiro Koizumi enraged several Asian countries by paying a visit to Tokyo's Yasukuni Shrine, where the Japanese who perished in conflicts are "memorialized and worshipped as deities," even troops who were executed as war criminals even if they have committed atrocities, the dead become kami.

The gion matsuri, or annual festival, is the most important annual event at any Japanese shrine today. During this festival, men and women from the community carry an image of the local shrine around the neighborhood to sanctify it as well as the people who live there. The mythology, as well as the associated customs and rites, continue to have an impact on current Japanese life and culture in a variety of ways. Many Japanese people follow Shinto ceremonies, although they are buried according to Buddhist rites. The Japanese reverence for nature, their emphasis on cleanliness and purification, and the discipline with which they approach play and work are all linked to Shinto and Buddhist traditions.

In Japan, there is a widespread statement that 80 percent of the population is Buddhist, 80 percent is Shinto, and 80 percent do not believe in any religion at all. The Japanese fusion of Buddhism and Shinto is more about doing certain things, such as meditating and visiting Buddhist temples and Shinto jinta, or shrines.

(Both sorts can be found in most homes.) Shinto weddings are the norm. The majority of Buddhist funerals are held.

Both religions emphasize ritual purification: before visiting a shrine, you wash your lips and hands. A lot of shrine visits and ceremonial blessings take place as well.

When the foundation for a new structure is laid, a ritual is held to appease and purify the kami that live there. New airplanes, like-new vehicles on a manufacturing assembly line, are cleansed before their first flight.

Toyota officials go three hours from their headquarters to the shrine of Amaterasu, the sun goddess, to present their newest vehicles.

Although the tales are no longer as prominent as they once were, Japanese tradition lives on—albeit with some uniquely Japanese changes. Before making a gift, a shrine visit still includes bathing, ringing a bell (to invite the kami), bowing twice, and clapping the hands twice. Few Japanese towns are without a Shinto shrine; there are over 80,000 of them across the country.

At a temple, you can still get your fate written on a sheet of paper. If it's nice, you keep it; if it's bad, you tie it up near the shrine and let the kami take care of it. The modern twist is that you can now purchase your fortune from a vending machine.

Conclusion

To conclude, let us summarise what we went through in this book.

The book starts with the myths about the origin of the nation of Japan.

The traditional tales, folktales, and beliefs that originated on the islands that make up the Japanese archipelago are compiled into what is known as Japanese mythology, which is the main issue of discussion in this book.

Shinto and Buddhist ideas serve as the cornerstones around which Japanese mythology is constructed. There has been engagement with Korea for thousands of years, as well as with the Ainu and Okinawan people, which all contributed to the development of Japanese mythology.

Both the Kojiki and the Nihon Shoki are essential literature for anybody interested in contemporary Japanese mythology. The Kojiki, also known as the "Record of Ancient Matters," is the oldest narrative of Japan's myths, legends, and history that has been preserved.

In addition, the Shintsh provides an analysis of the origins of Japanese gods and goddesses from a Buddhist point of view.

The Shinto pantheon is home to a plethora of kami, which is the Japanese word for "god(s)" or "spirits." The stories surrounding these kami are connected to the topography of the archipelago as well as to agriculturally-based forms of folk religion.

This book examines a variety of topics, including the primary deities, the current trends, the cultural significance, and the influence of the stories.

This book is a lane down the mythological memory that lets the interested minds acquaint with the past and recent mythological trends in Japan.

We hope that you got all the information that you wanted from this book.

Thank you, and good luck!